ON PURPOSE

Insight for New Leaders
and the Executives Who Develop Them

QUENTIN DAVIS

ON PURPOSE

Insight for New Leaders
and the Executives Who Develop Them

Quentin Davis

THE
FOUNDRY
PRESS

Published by The Foundry Press, an imprint of QTR Foundry

Upper Marlboro, MD

qtrfoundry.com

Intellectual Property

The ideas, frameworks, and models presented in this book are the original work of the author. They are intended for personal and organizational development and may not be reproduced, adapted, or used for commercial, training, or consulting purposes without written permission.

Disclaimer

This book reflects the author's experiences and perspectives. It is intended for educational and informational purposes only and does not constitute professional, legal, or financial advice. Readers are responsible for how they apply the material.

ISBN: 979-8-9956939-1-8

Cover and interior design by The Foundry Press

The Foundry Press is the publishing arm of QTR Foundry.

We publish books designed to sharpen leadership judgment, accelerate readiness, and strengthen execution through people, behavior, and structure.

Our work is grounded in a simple belief:

Organizations don't fail because of strategy.
They fail at the intersection of structure, alignment, and behavior.

That's where we operate.

Each title is built to deliver practical insight, disciplined thinking, and real-world application for leaders operating in complex environments.

This is not theory.

This is forged.

Learn more at: qtrfoundry.com

For Ebony, Drayper Jr., Zaria, & Destiny

DISCLAIMER

This is not a how—to guide.
It's a collection of hard-earned perspective—shaped
through experience, pressure, and real decisions.

Take what fits.
Apply it with discernment.
Refine it through your own leadership.

FOR THE EXPERIENCED LEADER

If you're a leader placing this in someone else's hands, do it **ON PURPOSE**.

These aren't theories. They're perspective—earned over time, often the hard way.

The kind most leaders don't get until they've already made the mistakes.

Use this to shorten that distance.

Not by over-explaining it. Not by turning it into a checklist.

But by giving it at the right moment— and letting it meet them where they are.

Some of it will land immediately.

Some of it won't make sense yet.

That's part of the process.

Leadership doesn't develop all at once. It reveals itself in moments— under pressure, in uncertainty, in decision.

This book is meant to sit close enough to be picked up in those moments.

It doesn't replace experience.

It sharpens it.

Your role isn't to walk them through every page. It's to:

◊   set the standard

◊   model the behavior

◊   create the environment where these ideas can take hold

If used that way, this won't just be something they read.

It will become something they return to.

And over time, something they lead with.

SPACE & GRACE

PERMISSION SLIP

You picked this book up and made it to page two.

Which means you aspire to be a better teammate and a better leader.

It's already inside of you.

It's there.

Give yourself permission.

Read this when you're ready to activate what's already inside of you.

Give yourself the space and grace to go at your own pace.

What follows isn't theory.
It's lived.
Take what fits.
Leave what doesn't.

Come back when you're ready.

X ______________________________________

Table of Contents

Space & Grace — Permission Slip

PART I
Where To Start

Pay Attention First

IT'S OK TO SHUT UP

LOOK

LISTEN

LEARN

The 3 L's

Most people confuse having a voice
with having something to say.

They speak early.
They speak often.
They speak to prove they belong in the room.

And in doing so—they miss the room entirely.

You were given two eyes. Two ears. One mouth.
That math is not accidental.

Yet watch how quickly we reverse it—
talking twice as much as we see.
Interrupting what we don't yet understand.
Announcing conclusions before the full picture ever arrives.

We mistake speed for intelligence.
Volume for leadership.
Certainty for competence.

The loudest person in the room is rarely the most dangerous.
The most dangerous person is the one who's watching.
They're not quiet because they lack confidence.
They're quiet because they're collecting data.
They're noticing patterns.
Learning how the game is actually played, not how it's explained
in meetings or framed in mission statements.

The student always goes further than the know-it-all.

Not because the student is smarter—
but because the student is willing to:

Look longer.
Listen harder.
Learn without performing while doing it.

Curiosity compounds.
Ego doesn't.

This isn't a call to silence.
It's a call to discipline. To restraint.
To the kind of presence that doesn't rush to be seen because it's
too busy understanding what matters.

Look first.
Listen longer.
Learn continuously.

If that feels uncomfortable-good.
Growth usually does.

Because once you've truly seen and heard what's in front of
you—
when you finally speak, you won't need to raise your voice.

The room will already be listening.

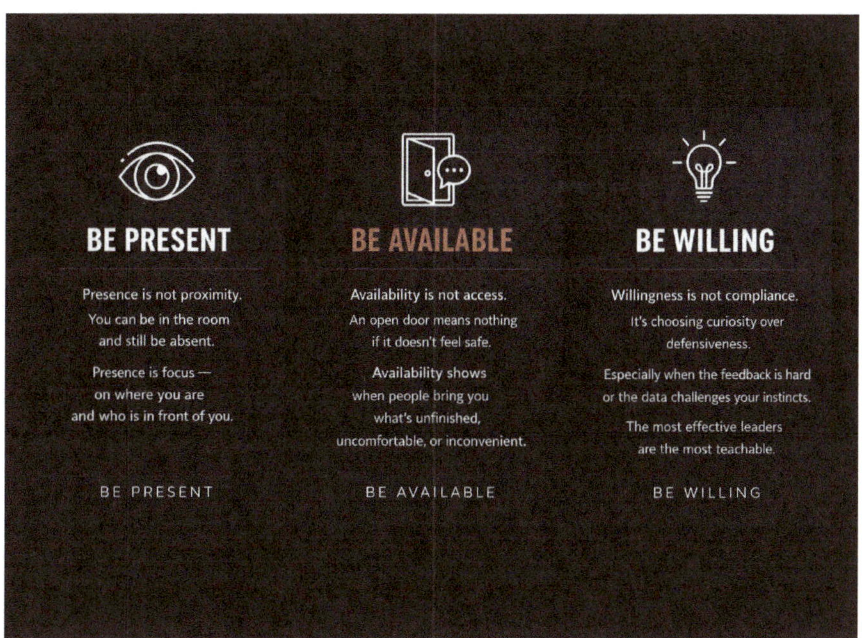

Presence is not proximity.

You can sit in every meeting and still be absent.
You can hear every word and still miss the point.

Presence is not about being seen—it's about being attentive enough to notice what others overlook.

The leaders people trust are rarely the most animated.
They're the ones who stay long enough in the moment to understand what's actually happening beneath the language.

Tone.
Hesitation.
What doesn't get said.

Presence is a discipline.

It costs focus. And it demands you set your distractions down before you ask others to pick anything up.

Availability is not access.

An open calendar doesn't mean an open leader.

People don't come forward because the door is unlocked—they come forward because it feels safe to walk through it.

Availability is emotional, not logistical. It's revealed in how you respond when someone brings you something unfinished, uncomfortable, or inconvenient.

Most people don't need answers. They need space. They need to know their voice won't be rushed, reframed, or weaponized.

Availability is what tells them this is a place where truth can survive.

Willingness is not compliance.

It's the quiet agreement to be changed by what you learn.

Willingness shows up when the feedback is clumsy, when the data contradicts your instincts, when the problem won't respect your title—especially when defensiveness would be easier.

The most effective leaders are not the most certain.
They are the most teachable.

They move because they are learning, not because they are reacting.

Bring it Together

Presence keeps you grounded.
Availability keeps you connected.
Willingness keeps you growing.

Together, they form a posture—not a personality.

A way of occupying space that tells people you're here to understand before you're here to be understood.

And once people see that posture consistently, something shifts.

They speak more honestly.
They listen more carefully.
They act with greater ownership.

Not because you told them to.

Because you showed them how.

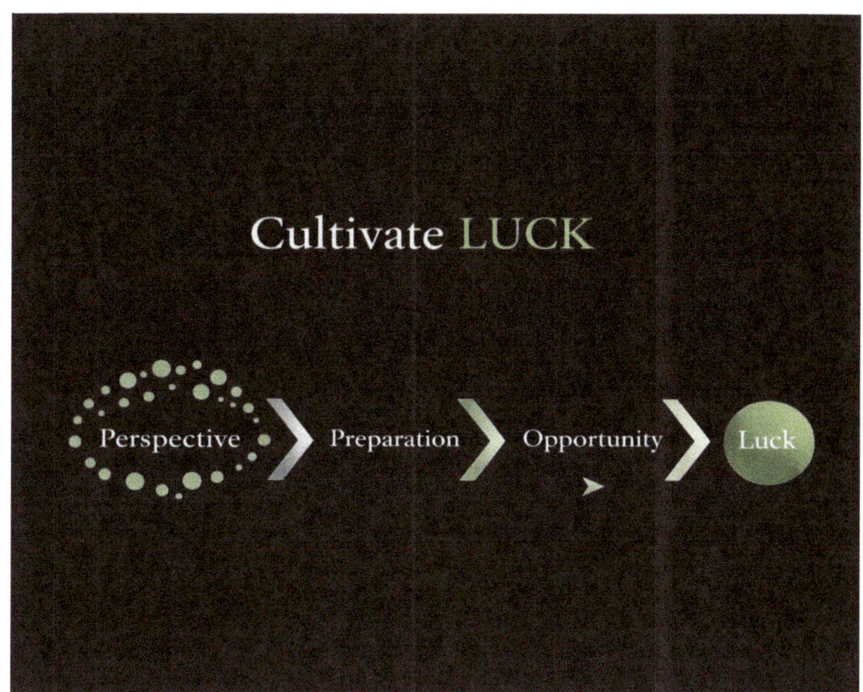

Luck is rarely random.

It's just misunderstood.

We talk about it as if it arrives unannounced—some external force that favors a few and ignores the rest.

But look closer and you'll notice a pattern.

Luck tends to show up where preparation has been waiting for it.

What people call luck is often something quieter.

It's preparation done quietly.
It's effort invested long before the payoff becomes visible.
Perspective shaped through experience.

It's the person who kept reading when no one was watching.
Kept asking questions when it would have been easier to nod along.
Kept building relationships without knowing when—or if—they'd matter.

Optimism isn't blind positivity.

It's the belief that your actions today are shaping access you haven't earned yet.

Opportunities don't arrive on demand.

They arrive on schedule—just not your schedule.
And when they do, they rarely announce themselves as opportunities.

They look like inconvenience.
Stretch.
Risk.

A decision you made two or three moves ago finally coming due.

This is why some people seem to be "in the right place at the right time" more often than others.
They've been preparing for rooms they haven't entered yet.
They've been practicing judgment so that when the moment comes, the decision doesn't feel foreign.

Luck is not a moment.

It's a sequence.

Perspective leads to preparation.
Preparation earns opportunity.
Opportunity rewards those who are ready to decide.

And what we call luck—what we admire from the outside—is simply the result of will and discipline exercised consistently over time.

Nothing mystical about it.

Just deliberate thought.
Deliberate action.
Deliberate decisions.

Make enough of those—
and eventually the world will call you lucky.

You'll know better.

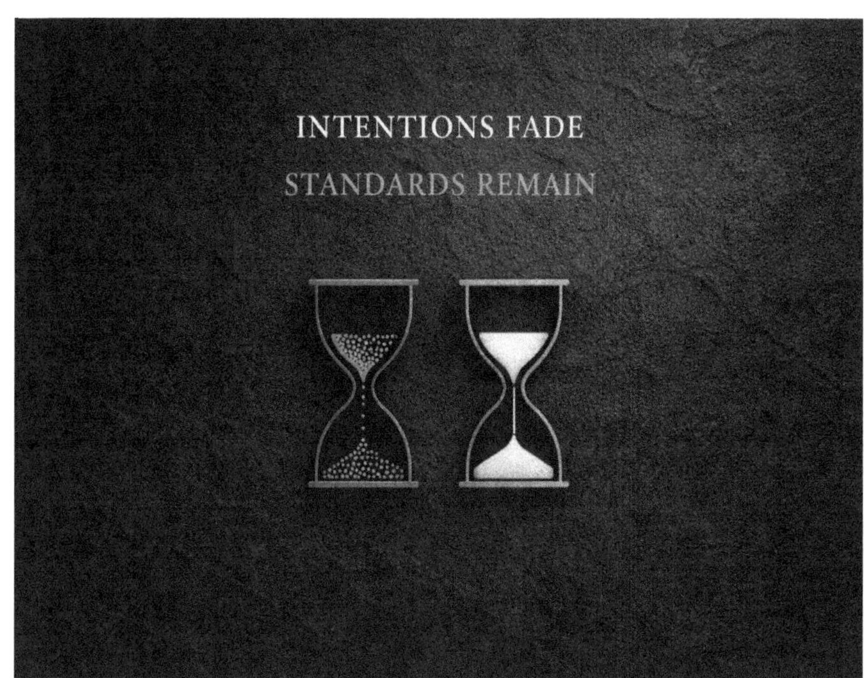

Standards Outlast Intentions

Most people mean well.

They intend to lead with integrity.
They intend to be fair.
They intend to show up differently once the title settles in.

Intentions feel good.
They're internal. Private. Clean.

But leadership is experienced externally—
And the outside world never interacts with what you meant to do.

It only lives with what you consistently allow.

**Intentions don't create clarity.
Standards do.**

When you step into a role you haven't occupied before, your intentions will be generous and your instincts incomplete.

That's normal.

What matters is what you anchor yourself to while you're still learning the terrain.

Standards become that anchor.

They decide what gets repeated and what gets corrected. They determine what earns recognition and what quietly erodes trust.
They speak long before you do.

People watch closely in the early days—not because they're skeptical, but because they're orienting themselves.

They're asking a simple question:

What actually matters here?

Not what's written.
Not what's promised.
What's enforced.
What's tolerated.
What passes without comment.

Every gap between intention and standard teaches something. And the lesson is rarely the one you hoped to deliver.

Good intentions create potential.
Standards create reality.

This is where new leaders often hesitate.

Setting standards feels heavy.
Final.

Like a declaration before you're fully certain you deserve the authority behind it. Authority doesn't come from certainty.

It comes from consistency.

Clear standards don't require you to have all the answers.

They require you to be honest about:

What you will protect.
what you will challenge.
What you will not ignore.

Over time, people stop asking who you are as
a leader. They already know.

They've been living inside the standards you've set.

Your standards matter more than your intent, your talent, or
your title—it's what will define your leadership long after the
learning curve flattens.

PART II
Forging Forward

Absorb. Decide. Move.

Are You the Sponge?

Leadership absorbs impact before it distributes clarity.

If you're doing it right, the pressure doesn't land evenly—it comes to you first.

Teams bring confusion, frustration, unfinished thinking, and unspoken tension. Not because they're incapable—but because that's the work. Someone has to hold it long enough to understand what matters and what doesn't.
That someone is usually the leader.

Like a sponge, you take on what others can't carry yet.

You absorb misalignment before it hardens into conflict. You catch gaps before they widen. You deal with issues while they're still manageable—often invisibly, often without credit. That work doesn't look heroic. It looks ordinary—but it keeps things from breaking.

There's another side to the sponge that rarely gets mentioned.

Leadership isn't just about taking things in—it's about restoring order.

Eventually, it has to scrub.

Addressing performance. Naming standards. Saying the thing that makes the room quiet. This isn't aggression—it's care with a backbone. it's part of it.

Discipline isn't the opposite of service; it's a part of it.
And even the best sponge can't stay saturated forever.

If you never wring it out, it stops working. That's not weakness—it's physics.

Leaders who last understand this. They step away long enough to recover perspective, to regain clarity, to remember who they are outside the problems they carry. Durability isn't endurance at all costs. It's knowing when renewal is non-negotiable.

There's a final truth most people don't talk about.

Every sponge is temporary.

Your role is not to absorb everything forever. It's to serve long enough, well enough, that the system no longer needs you in the same way. Someone else will take your place. That's not failure. That's completion.

Because in the end, the sponge is a tool—not a monument.

To lead is to serve.
To serve is to absorb.
And to do both well is to know when it's time to let go.

If you can make peace with that, you'll lead with humility instead of attachment—and your impact will outlast your position.

Impact doesn't announce itself.
It accumulates.

Walk into any team, any room, any culture—and you can feel it.
The energy.
The pace.
The seriousness.
 The drift.

None of it happened by chance. It is the residue of how time, effort, and attitude have been spent there, day after day.

Time is the most honest signal you send.

Not what you say matters—but where you stay. What you linger on. What you rush past. People notice where your attention goes, because attention is commitment made visible.

Time tells the truth about priorities long before words ever do.

Effort is what gives intention its weight.

Desired outcomes don't materialize because they're deserved. They arrive when someone is willing to do the work others avoid—thinking more deeply, preparing more thoroughly, following through when the momentum fades.

Effort is rarely dramatic, but it is always decisive. It's the difference between movement and progress.

And **attitude**—attitude changes everything.

Not optimism. Not cheerfulness.
Attitude as posture.

How you enter pressure.
How you respond to friction.
Whether your presence steadies the room or unsettles it.

Attitude determines whether your time and effort multiply—or cancel each other out.
This is where leaders often miscalculate.

They underestimate how closely they are watched. How their impatience becomes permission. How their inconsistency becomes confusion. How their composure—or lack of it—sets the ceiling for everyone else.

Time, effort, and attitude are never neutral.

They either elevate the environment—or quietly erode it.

Teams don't rise to ambition.
They settle into what's modeled consistently.

If your impact feels limited, look there first.

Not at your authority.
Not at your title.

At how you're spending your time, how fully you're investing effort, and the attitude you bring into the room when it counts.

Because long before people follow your direction—
They absorb your example.

And that's the impact that lasts.

Adding Vulnerability to Your Toolbox

Vulnerability is often misunderstood because it's talked about too casually.

It gets confused with exposure. With oversharing. With emotion that hasn't processed.

That version of vulnerability isn't leadership—it's release.
And release, by itself, doesn't build trust.

Useful vulnerability is deliberate.

It's the willingness to be seen without surrendering the work.
To acknowledge uncertainty without abandoning responsibility.
To say, "I don't have the answer yet," while still owning the obligation to find it.

This matters most for leaders stepping into unfamiliar territory.

When you're new to the role, the pressure to perform certainty is strong. To fill silence quickly. To project confidence before it's fully earned.

People don't need you to be flawless.
They need you to be honest enough to name reality and steady enough to hold it.

Vulnerability creates permission.

It tells others they don't have to hide confusion or pretend progress. It lowers defensiveness. It opens dialogue. And when done well, it doesn't weaken authority—it strengthens it by replacing distance with credibility.

There's discipline here.

Vulnerability is not about revealing everything.
It's about revealing what's useful.

What helps the team move.
What invites contribution.
What signals humility without creating instability.

Strong leaders understand this balance.

They don't posture vulnerability to be liked.
They use it to build trust, widen perspective, and invite ownership.
They model learning in real time—without losing command of the moment.

And in doing so, they remind everyone that leadership isn't about having all the answers—it's about charting the course toward them.

Not every moment calls for vulnerability.
But when the moment does, avoiding it costs more than using it.

Over time, people don't remember how polished you were.

They remember whether you were real enough to make the work possible.

That's why vulnerability belongs in the toolbox.

Not as a default.

As a choice.

The Thin Lines **of Leadership**

Leadership rarely fails at the edges.
It erodes when standards drift.

The distance between what strengthens a team and what damages it is often narrow—thin enough that you can cross it without noticing.

That's why leadership requires discernment more than intention.
The difference isn't always in the action itself—
It's in the posture behind it.

Every strength you rely on has a line.

On one side, it serves you.
On the other, its starts to distort and work against you.
And most of the time, the drift is subtle.

Start with **accountability**.

There's a line between owning outcomes and deflecting blame to others.

Leaders who refuse accountability erode trust.
Leaders who deflect blame erode their credibility.
Giving yourself grace keeps you from crossing that line.

Own what's yours.
Learn from it.
Then let it go.

Passion has its line, too.

Drive and commitment are essential. They move people forward. But when passion slips into emotional reactivity, clarity disappears.

Decisions get personal.
Feedback feels like threat.

Staying grounded is what allows passion to remain useful. It keeps intensity from becoming instability—and ensures your energy lifts the room instead of unsettling it.

Confidence walks another narrow path.

Teams need leaders who believe in themselves. They also need leaders who remember the work is bigger than them.

Confidence becomes arrogance the moment it stops making room for others.

Humility isn't self-doubt—it's self-awareness.
It keeps confidence from becoming entitlement and authority from becoming isolation.

And **ambition**—

Ambition may be the thinnest line of all.

Healthy ambition sharpens focus and pulls the future closer. Toxic ambition justifies shortcuts, excuses behavior, and tolerates what should never be normalized.

Self-awareness is the safeguard here.
The ability to pause and ask: "What am I willing to trade to get there—and is it worth it?"

These lines aren't theoretical.
You'll cross them. More than once.

The goal isn't perfection.

It's recognition. Catching yourself early.
Surrounding yourself with people solid enough to tell you when you've drifted. Welcoming feedback before drift becomes necessary.

Leadership isn't about avoiding mistakes.
It's about noticing sooner when you're close to the edge.

The thinner the line—
The greater the responsibility to walk it carefully.

PART III
Your Time is Now

Show Up Like It Matters

Stay Formidable

Formidable leaders don't announce themselves.

They don't compete for attention, dominance, or control.
They don't need to be the smartest voice, the loudest presence, or the most intimidating figure in the room.
Those signals are obvious—and obvious power is rarely the most effective.

Formidability shows up differently.

It's the quiet confidence that comes from knowing where influence actually lives.
The discipline to listen before speaking. The restraint to wait while others rush.
The awareness to understand the room—not just the conversation happening on the surface, but the currents underneath it.

Formidable leaders know their angle.

They understand relationships as leverage—not in a manipulative sense, but in a human one.
They recognize that decisions move through trust, not titles. That progress depends on timing as much as conviction.
That presence, when steady, shapes outcomes long after the meeting ends.

This kind of strength isn't performative.

It's rooted in self-awareness—the ability to regulate yourself under pressure.
In situational awareness—the skill of adjusting without losing your footing.
In confidence that doesn't need to prove itself. In humility that keeps learning possible.
In vulnerability that builds credibility instead of instability.

Above all, formidable leaders know how to work with people—not around them, not over them.

They negotiate relationships thoughtfully. They create alignment without force. They move systems forward without creating resistance.

Formidable doesn't mean feared. It means respected.
And respect, sustained over time, is what makes influence durable.

If you can stay formidable—steady, discerning, and grounded—you won't need to assert your authority.

Your presence will already be shaping the room.

INFLUENCE UP
Reduce Risk
Increase Clarity · Earn Trust
COLLABORATE ACROSS
Alignment · Relationships
Shared Progress
LEADERSHIP
COLLABORATE ACROSS
Alignment · Relationships
Shared Progress
INSPIRE DOWN
Consistency · Standards · Presence
Miss one angle. The system breaks.

Working the Angles

Leadership doesn't operate in a straight line.

It moves in directions—up, down, and across—and your effectiveness depends on whether you can navigate all three without losing credibility in any of them. Most leaders are taught to focus on one. The work demands all three, at the same time.

Influence up is about trust, not proximity to power.

Titles don't grant influence upward—judgment does. Clarity does. Consistency does. Those above you aren't looking for flattery or friction. They're watching for discernment.

Can you see the full picture?
Can you carry weight without needing to be carried?

Influence up is earned when your presence reduces risk rather than introduces it.

Inspiration down is built, not assigned.

People don't follow because they have to.
They follow when they believe you see them, protect standards, and mean what you say.
Inspiration is the byproduct of credibility—of showing up prepared, making hard decisions with care, and holding yourself to the same expectations you place on others.

Authority may get compliance. Trust earns commitment.

Collaboration across is where leadership matures.

Peers are not obstacles. They're multipliers.
The ability to work laterally—to align interests, negotiate priorities, and move without formal authority—is often the difference between momentum and stall.

Leaders who ignore this axis isolate themselves. Leaders who master it extend their reach far beyond their role.

If one of these directions breaks down, the whole system feels it.

Influence without inspiration becomes manipulation. Inspiration without collaboration becomes insular. Collaboration without influence becomes noise.

The most effective leaders are fluent in all three.

They pause to assess where the relationship needs work. They adjust without defensiveness. They re-engage with intention.

Not because they're unsure—but because they understand this is the ongoing discipline of leadership.

This is **the work beneath the work.**

No shortcuts. No substitutions. Just steady attention to the relationships that make movement possible.

BARRIER AHEAD.
QUESTION WHY.
OVER
THROUGH
AROUND
ANALYZE. ASSESS. DECIDE.
KEEP MOVING.

Barriers: Over, Through, or Around

Barriers are not interruptions to leadership.

They are confirmations of it.

Every team, every effort, every meaningful pursuit will encounter them. And rarely are they accidental.

Most barriers exist because someone before you learned something the hard way—or because risk demanded restraint. The leader's first responsibility is not to react, but to understand.

Question why the barrier exists.
Analyze the situation without ego.
Assess the risk without fear.

Not every obstacle is meant to be challenged in the same way, and not every barrier is yours to break.

Leadership is measured by discernment long before it's measured by action.

Once you understand the terrain, the choice becomes yours.

Sometimes leadership requires going **over** the barrier—rising above limitations with vision, resolve, and the willingness to carry others with you.

Sometimes it requires going **through**—doing the hard, unglamorous work of dismantling what stands in the way, piece by piece, with patience and endurance.

And sometimes the most responsible move is going **around**— finding another path forward without unnecessary damage, delay, or cost to the people you lead.

There is no universal answer.

What matters is that the decision is intentional, informed, and owned.

Indecision stalls momentum. Avoidance erodes confidence. But movement—deliberate movement—builds trust.

Teams don't expect perfection from their leaders.
They expect clarity.
They expect progress.
They expect you to keep going.

Whatever you choose—over, through, or around—choose it with purpose.

And then move.

Because leadership isn't proven by the absence of barriers.
It's revealed by how you lead others through them.

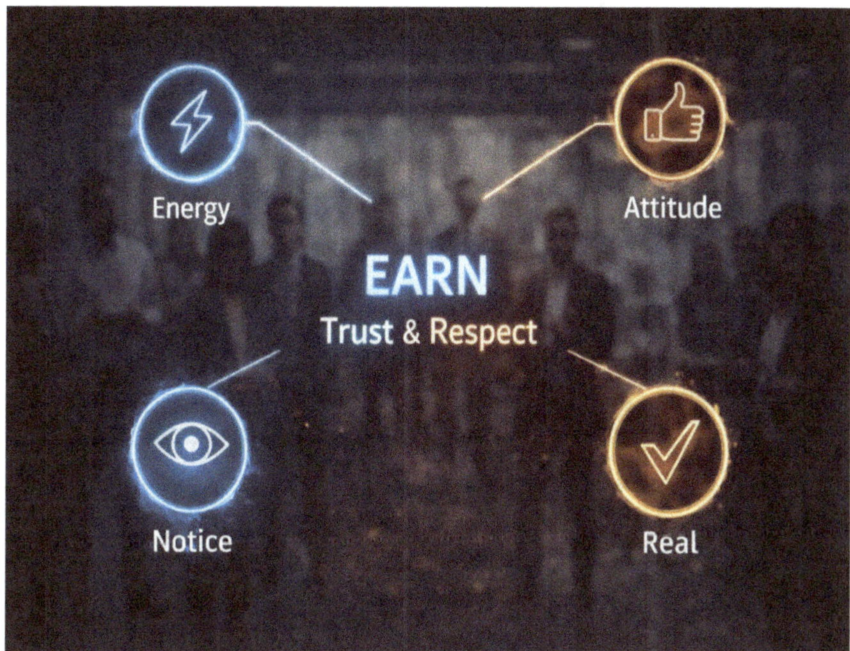

EARN

Trust and respect are not granted with a title.

They are earned—continuously, visibly, and without shortcuts.

Every leader lives in a glass house. Your energy, your attitude, how real you are, and whether you notice the people doing the work around you are always on display. Nothing is hidden for long. People are paying attention, even when you think they're not.

This is the quiet work of leadership.

And it can be understood through four signals that never stop transmitting.

Energy.

Your energy enters the room before you do.

It's felt immediately—high or low, open or closed, constructive or corrosive.

Energy is not a soft concept. It's tangible. It affects momentum, problem-solving, and morale.

Negative energy, even when unspoken, becomes a drag on performance. Positive energy, when genuine, creates lift.

The overlooked truth is this: energy is one of the few leadership assets fully within your control every day. You've already proven you can deliver results. Don't let unmanaged energy undermine the credibility you've worked to build. People are drawn to leaders whose presence steadies the environment, not destabilizes it.

Attitude.

If energy sets the temperature, attitude sets the tone.

Your attitude—how you carry yourself under pressure, how you frame challenges, how you speak about others—shapes how effective you are at motivating a team. It reflects your outlook, your intent, and your maturity. While emotions are human, attitude is a choice. And it's one that belongs to you alone.

Leaders lose ground the moment they allow circumstances—or other people—to control their attitude. Teams feel that loss immediately. Attitude signals whether you are someone worth following when things are difficult, not just when they're easy.

Real (Authentic).

People are remarkably good at detecting what isn't real.

In an age where information is accessible and transparency is unavoidable, disingenuous leadership doesn't survive long. Being real isn't about oversharing or abandoning standards—it's about alignment. Between what you say and what you do. Between who you are privately and how you show up publicly.

Authenticity creates climate. A climate where feedback is welcomed. Where truth is safe. Where leaders don't pretend to have all the answers, but take responsibility for finding them. Being REAL requires humility—the confidence to admit what you don't know, and the discipline to put the work above your ego.

It's exhausting to be fake. And one slip erodes more credibility than silence ever could.

Noticing.

Noticing is the most underestimated leadership skill.

People are motivated in different ways. Some value public recognition. Others value a quiet acknowledgment that their effort was seen. What matters isn't the method—it's the attention. Two words, offered sincerely

—*thank you*—carry more weight than most leaders realize.

When you notice individual contributions, you build equity in trust. You reinforce purpose. You remind people they are there because they matter, not just because they have to be. Over time, this directly impacts the quality of output. People don't give their best to environments that don't see them.

This is why EARN matters.

You cannot demand trust.
You cannot enforce respect.
You cannot shortcut influence.

They are earned—through your energy, your attitude, how real you are, and your willingness to notice the people who make the work possible.

Coercion may produce compliance. Earning trust produce commitment.

And leadership without trust and respect isn't leadership at all. It's position—fragile, temporary, and easily resisted.

EARN it. Every day.

PART IV
Bring Em' With You
Bring Others Forward

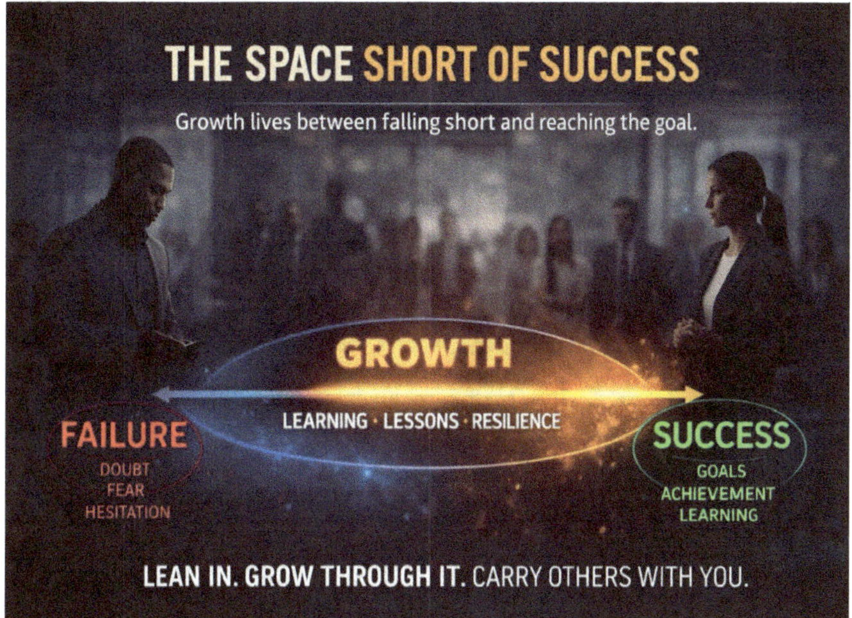

The Space Short of Success

Success is rarely a clean arrival.

Most of the time, it's preceded by something quieter—
falling short. Missing the mark. Coming close and still
coming up empty. What matters in those moments isn't
the outcome itself, but the mindset that's cultivated in its
wake.

Every leader, whether they intend to or not, teaches their team
how to interpret those moments.

Some environments treat falling short as failure. They allow
doubt to take root. Confidence erodes. Risk narrows. People
begin to play not to lose instead of playing to win. Over time,
effort becomes conservative, creativity shrinks, and potential
goes dormant.

Other environments see something different.

They understand that **growth** lives in the space between failure
and success.

That the distance matters. That lessons learned under pressure
shape better judgment, sharper instincts, and stronger teams.

These leaders don't ignore results—but they refuse to let missed targets define the people who aimed high.

This distinction is critical.

Fear of so-called failure breeds hesitation. It teaches people to protect themselves instead of the work. But when leaders frame falling short as part of growth, something changes. Teams stay engaged. Ownership increases. Confidence becomes resilient rather than fragile.

Not everyone chooses this path.

Many people settle for the hand life deals them. Few commit to overcoming obstacles with intention. Fewer still lead others through those moments with clarity and steadiness. But that's exactly where leadership reveals its character.

The mindset you cultivate determines who stays invested.

It determines whether people lean in or pull back when things don't go as planned.
Whether they grow or shrink under pressure.
Whether your culture becomes cautious—or capable of something more.

Growth isn't accidental.

It's a byproduct of how leaders respond when success isn't immediate. Of how they speak in disappointment. Of what they reinforce after effort doesn't pay off—yet.

We don't fail.

We **GROW**.

And the leaders who truly understand that don't just say it.

They live it—especially when it's hardest to do so.

Be Consistent & Stay Humble

Momentum can lie to you.

Early wins, visible progress, and growing confidence have a way of convincing leaders they've arrived—when in reality, they've just been noticed.

This is where leadership quietly shifts from earned credibility to assumed authority if you're not careful.

Consistency is what keeps that from happening.

People don't trust leaders because of what they say once. They trust them because of what they do repeatedly. How you show up on ordinary days matters more than how you perform in defining moments.

Consistency removes confusion. It tells people what to expect from you —and whether it's safe to follow.

Humility keeps consistency honest.

Without humility, ambition hardens. Communication becomes one-directional. Care turns transactional. Leaders start mistaking visibility for value and influence for entitlement.

Humility interrupts that drift.

It reminds you that leadership is still service, even when responsibility grows.

Ambition is not the problem.

Without vision, no one moves. People need to know where you're going and why it matters. But ambition must be paired with clarity and restraint. When vision isn't communicated well, it becomes distance. When it isn't shared, it becomes self-serving.

Communication is the bridge.

Words shape relationships.
They set tone.
They reinforce standards.

Poor communication erodes trust faster than most mistakes. Strong leaders never stop sharpening this skill—not to control narratives, but to keep reality aligned across the team.

And then there's care.

No one gives their best effort to leaders they don't believe care about them. Not their output. Not their well-being. Not their growth. Care isn't softness—it's **currency.**
It's the difference between compliance and commitment.

Consistency proves who you are.

Humility keeps you accountable for it.

Together, they prevent leadership from becoming performative. They anchor ambition. They protect culture. And they ensure that as others rise with you, they aren't carrying the weight alone.

At this stage, leadership isn't about being impressive.

It's about being reliable.

And staying grounded enough to remember why people trusted you in the first place.

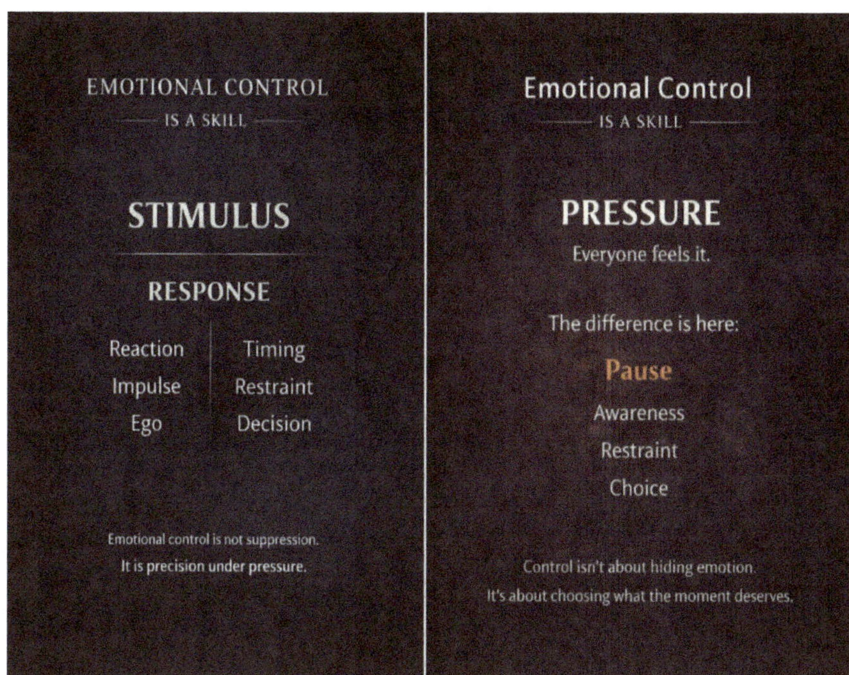

Emotional Control Is a Leadership Skill

There's a quiet misconception that emotional control is something you either *have* or *don't* have.

That it's tied to temperament. Personality. Wiring.

It's not.

Emotional control is a **skill**.

And like every other leadership skill, it is learned, practiced, tested, and refined.

Leaders are human. You feel frustration. Pressure. Doubt. Disappointment. The difference is not *whether* you feel— it's **what you do with it.**

Your title does not excuse emotional volatility.
Your stress does not justify emotional leakage.
And your intentions do not override the impact of your reactions.

In moments of uncertainty, people don't look to your résumé.

They look to your **regulation**.

When you stay composed, you create space for others to think.
When you remain steady, you signal safety.
When you choose restraint, you preserve trust.

Emotional control does not mean being cold. It means being **disciplined**.
It means knowing when to pause instead of react. When to ask instead of accuse.
When to absorb instead of discharge.

Leaders who lack emotional control often call it *passion*.
Teams experience it as **instability**. And instability erodes credibility faster than incompetence ever could.

This is where maturity shows up.

Not in calm moments—but when things don't go your way.
When timelines slip.
When people disappoint you.
When pressure tightens.

That's when leadership becomes visible.

If you can't manage your emotions, you will eventually ask your team to manage them *for* you.
That is not leadership. That is burden.

Emotional control is not about suppression.

It's about **command**.

Command of self.
Command of tone.
Command of presence.

And like every meaningful leadership skill—

it is practiced **ON PURPOSE.**

POUR INTO THEM &
YOUR ACTIONS

P O U R

PRIDE   OWNERSHIP   URGENCY   RESULTS

Pour into the work. Pour into the people.
Success multiplies in the patterns you reinforce.

Pour Into 'Em & Your Actions

You didn't get here by accident.

You've been successful to this point because you pour yourself into what you do. Not casually. Not selectively. Fully. You take pride in your work. You own your decisions. You move with urgency when it matters. And you stay focused on results—not recognition.

That combination is rare. And it's worth naming.

POUR isn't a slogan. It's a pattern.

Pride means your name is on the work whether anyone's watching or not.

Ownership means you don't outsource responsibility when things get uncomfortable.

Urgency means you respect time—yours and everyone else's.

Results mean you understand effort only matters if it moves something forward.

This mindset is why people trust you with more.

But here's where leadership sharpens.

At this stage, pouring into the work isn't enough. You're now responsible for pouring into **people**—through your actions, not your intentions.

What you model becomes permission.
What you tolerate becomes culture.
What you invest in multiplies.

Teams don't follow words.
They follow behavior.

When people see you take pride, they raise their standards.
When they see you own outcomes, they stop hiding.
When they feel urgency without panic, they move with purpose.
When results are clear, trust compounds.

This is how success becomes repeatable.

Not because everything goes right—but because your approach is consistent. Because you pour into what matters. Because you understand that leadership isn't about intensity in moments, but commitment over time.

Keep pouring.

Into the work.

Into the people.

Into the standards you live by.

When you do, success stops being something you chase.

It becomes something you create—again and again—through how you show up.

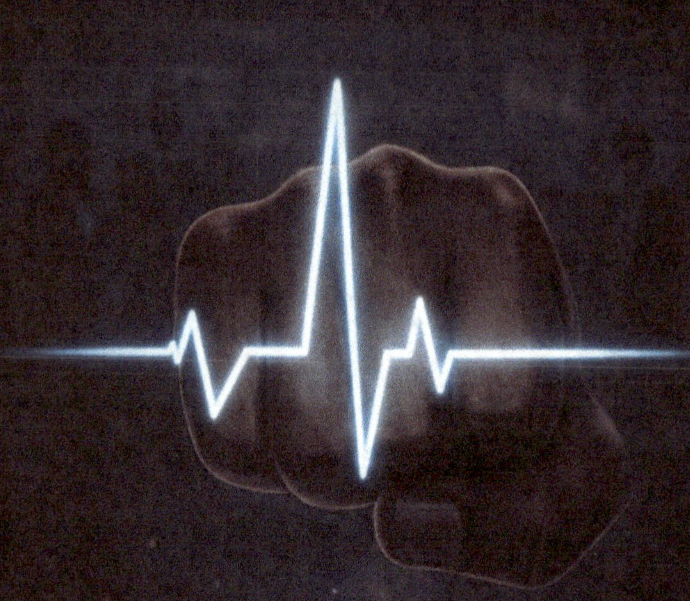

ELEVATE THE FREQUENCY
ON PURPOSE

There will always be noise.

Doubt. Criticism. Fatigue.

People who go low when pressure rises. That's not a surprise—that's the environment. Leadership doesn't exempt you from it. Leadership *responds* to it.

When the frequency around you drops, you don't match it.

You **set** it.

Elevating the frequency isn't about optimism for optimism's sake.

It's about presence.

About choosing clarity when confusion would be easier. About bringing steadiness into moments that tempt reaction.

Your energy—how you show up, how you listen, how you speak, how you move—becomes the reference point whether you intend it to or not.

So be intentional.

Not loud.
Not performative.

Intentional.

Your team will take cues from how you carry pressure. From how you treat resistance. From whether you shrink, harden, or rise when things don't go as planned. This is where influence stops being positional and starts being personal.

You don't elevate the frequency by accident.

You do it through choices.

By refusing to let negativity dictate direction.
By responding instead of reacting.
By taking meaningful action when others hesitate.
By understanding that energy, once released, multiplies.

This isn't about leaving things to chance.

It's about deciding—every day—what standard you're willing to live and lead by.

When they go low, you don't follow.

You lift the room.
You lift the people.
You lift the work.

And you do it—

ON PURPOSE.

TAKE THIS FURTHER

If this book resonated, don't let it sit.

The ideas in this book are designed to be applied—individually and across teams.

This book is the starting point.
The real work happens in the room.

QTR Foundry partners with leaders and executive teams to:
• Strengthen alignment under pressure
• Elevate leadership behavior
• Accelerate execution through trust and clarity

Through immersive labs, executive sessions, and advisory partnerships, we help organizations build leaders who can execute—not just manage.

If you're serious about developing leaders who can translate strategy into action, this work scales beyond the page.

Bring it into your organization.

qdavis@qtrfoundry.com
qtrfoundry.com

About the Author

Quentin Davis is a Human Capital Executive with more than 20 years of experience leading workforce strategy, organizational transformation, and culture change across complex, high-stakes environments. He specializes in aligning people strategy with business objectives—driving measurable performance, strengthening leadership capability, and building cultures where accountability, trust, and results coexist. He holds a Master's Degree in Organizational Development & Leadership from The University of the Incarnate Word.